Wor

A Beginner's

MW01519873

!

the World

By: Sarah Dunsworth

Table of Contents

Introduction

In the past 100 years or so, travel innovations have opened up the world like never before. It is now possible to find oneself in a completely different country and culture within just a few hours. While the distance between us has become smaller, cultural differences and misunderstandings can remind us very quickly that we are actually worlds apart. Taking the time to learn about the people and culture of the country that you are planning to visit can make your experience rich and rewarding...and ignoring the local customs might mean that not only is your visit not all that it could be, but that you will most likely leave a trail of offense and stereotypes in your wake.

I spent 12 years living in South America, and during my time there, I both committed and witnessed cultural "faux pas" that sometimes made me wish that no one actually knew what country I hailed from. One particular "practice" that nearly all North Americans engage in is raising their voice when the person they are speaking to doesn't understand them.

The scenario is almost always the same. "Expat Mike" is attempting to negotiate a purchase, order a meal or ask for directions in English. The person he is speaking to either doesn't speak English or has a very limited grasp of the language. Not only can Mike not communicate his wishes, but he cannot understand the answer. Cue the raised voice and S-L-O-W speech. This implies that the person is he speaking to is not only deaf but also mentally deficient—neither of which is accurate. As the conversation continues, Mike becomes louder and louder, and the embarrassment level grows and grows, until he finally storms off, complaining loudly about the "stupid natives", who have done their best to help him and are left with the taste of "Ugly American" in their mouth.

This guide is designed to provide the reader with common etiquette practices in different countries around the world. Since we cannot cover every country, we have chosen to divide our guide into regions that are popular travel destinations. While different countries have their own practices, chances are that the social norms are very similar and you will be able to use the guide that we've given you and have a successful visit.

The key to a wonderful time in your host country is simple. Pay attention to what is happening around you, don't assume that you know how to do things the "right way", and be willing to absorb the rich and vibrant culture around you, ensuring that you go home just a little bit different than you were when you left. You will not change your host country in any discernable way...however, it can change you if you are willing to allow it.

Central and Latin America

Central and Latin America is comprised of the region that runs from Mexico, which is just over the border from the US, to the tip of Chile. The people are warm and inviting. The culture is people and experience-oriented rather than time-oriented. It is a very relaxed culture (except when they are behind the wheel of a car, but that's another story!) and the people are friendly and open.

Social Norms

North American culture is, as a rule, time-oriented. We make appointments, and we expect that the meeting will happen at the appointed time. In the Latin American culture, time is a fluid concept. Even when an appointed time is set, it is "understood" that the time is not fixed, but rather a general approximation of when the event will take place--and it's possible that it won't take place at all—something more important may come up. Mañana is the "understood" word for "tomorrow". It's one of the many Spanish words that has permeated the English lexicon, and everyone knows what it means...or thinks they do. The truth is that mañana does not actually mean "tomorrow". It is a general word that just means "not right now". It might happen tomorrow...or the next day...or never. But it won't happen right now. If you absolutely need something to happen at an appointed time, when you make your arrangements, emphasize that the event needs to happen "hora Americana" (Gringo time, essentially). This is still no guarantee, but it will at least help people to understand your expectations.

The Latin American culture places a high emphasis on relationship. No relationship with someone, essentially means that they simply don't exist and deserve no acknowledgment. Relationship to a North American mind means a friend, acquaintance or relative, however in the Latin culture it is much simpler. A relationship can be established simply through eye contact or a smile. The key is that once the relationship has been established, there is now the expectation of give-and-take. When you are out and about, taking the time to establish relationships with the people you are interacting with, it will result in a much more pleasant experience.

Meeting and Greeting

The Latin culture is very relational, and how you greet someone is very important. Always begin your greeting with buenos dias (good morning), buenas tardes (good afternoon) or buenos noches (good evening). This applies to everyone from shopkeepers to friends, and it is considered rude to immediately begin a conversation or request without doing so. Traditionally, Latin Americans greet one another with a "besito" (literally "little kiss") on the cheek. When entering a room, it is very important to greet every person in the room, even if the meeting or event that you are attending has already begun. If you do not know the person well, a handshake is acceptable, but usually only once. After that, you have established a relationship, and a besito is the acceptable greeting. Men do not have to besito other men (although you will see it—typically they do so to relatives, but not friends) but women do so with other women. Not greeting someone properly is an extreme breach of etiquette, and is taken very seriously.

Meal Time!

There are three main meals in the Latin culture, and all are usually taken together. This means that a business will probably shut down from 1:00-2:00 so that all of the employees can eat lunch together, and if you walk into a store it is perfectly acceptable for you to have to wait until they are finished before they help you. Depending on the nature of the business and how well they know you, they may ask you to join them. By all means do so! "Cafecito" ("little coffee") occurs about 10:00 in the morning. As most people in Latin America do not eat breakfast, this is their first meal of the day. Drinking coffee is a social event. When we first moved to Ecuador, I could not find travel mugs anywhere. I asked an Ecuadorian friend why they didn't sell them and she said, "Why would anyone want to drink coffee alone while driving in the car?" During cafecito there will typically be coffee (Rarely percolated or drip—most people drink "café con leche" which is instant coffee that they add liberal amounts of milk and sugar too. If you are a coffee snob like I am...I'm sorry. You'll get used to it. Sort of.), pancitos ("little breads"), jam and butter.

Lunch is the main meal of the day. It is usually eaten between 1:00 and 3:00, and consists of juice, soup, a main meal, a small dessert, and coffee or tea. The main portion of the meal will be white rice—meat is a garnish rather than the main dish. You will usually get a small salad (a lettuce leaf, a slice of tomato and an onion is the most common, with a vinaigrette dressing), corn or potatoes and a vegetable of some sort. The traditional diet is very heavy in carbohydrates, although it does vary from country to country.

Dinner is usually eaten sometime between 7:00 and 9:00 in the evening and generally consists of a cup of coffee and a pancito.

*It is important to note that when dining out, most restaurants are unable or unwilling to accommodate food allergies. If you ask a server if the meal has gluten in it, for example, he will tell you what he thinks you want to hear, as he is simply trying to be helpful. Chances are he doesn't even know what you're talking about. If you have food sensitivities, it is best to take a supply of food that you know you can eat, as there is little available in the stores to accommodate you. Also, food products are not required to have their allergens on their packaging as they are here in the US.

Street food is readily available no matter where you are in Latin America. It's going to smell really good...be really cheap...and probably make you really sick. Trust us—it's not worth it. Be especially careful with juices, ice cream and anything else that is not cooked. We once had a visitor who bought herself a glass of juice from a street vendor about 12 hours before she was scheduled to fly home. Needless to say, it was the most miserable plane ride of her entire life.

Bottled water is available at every little store, from people in the middle of the street, and most likely at your hotel/hostel. Even in places like Quito, Ecuador, which is considered a "first world city", it is not safe to drink the tap water. The filters that come with most water bottles sold here in the US are not for biological hazards, and will not protect you from all of the "swimmies" in the water in Latin America. If you cannot get bottled water, you can purify your own either by boiling it for 20 minutes or by putting one tablespoon of chlorine bleach in a gallon of water. If you order water in a restaurant, it will be bottled water. If you are in a larger restaurant that caters to tourists, it will be safe to have ice in your drink—otherwise it is not recommended.

Most Latin American countries are famous for their abundant fruits and vegetables. By all means try them! The general rule is that if you can peel it (bananas, oranges, etc.) it is safe to eat without disinfecting. All other fruits and veggies (apples, strawberries, carrots, etc.) need to be disinfected first. There are products sold that you can use (Kil-ol is a popular one) or you can use one tablespoon of bleach in a gallon of water and soak your produce for about 20 minutes.

Talking on the Phone

Most people have cell phones, and cell phone etiquette is relatively loose. There is really no "unacceptable" time to answer the phone. This means that you will see (and hear) people answering their phones in church, during movies, and in government buildings. Even if there are signs directing that no phones are to be used, people will still use them, and because it is considered rude to point out to someone that they are being rude, most of the time no one will call them on it.

Gift Giving

Gifts are never to be opened in front of the giver. This is so that if the recipient doesn't like the gift, there is no loss of face on either side. Even at children's birthday parties and events where we would expect the gift to be opened, such as wedding and baby showers, the gifts are taken home and opened later.

Body Language

Your body language speaks volumes about you, and will tell people far more than your words do. Gestures such as the middle finger convey the same message as they do in the US and are considered just as rude there as they are here. The concept of "personal space" is virtually unheard of, and you will find that people are standing almost on top of you in line. If you leave the "assured clear distance" that we are accustomed to here in the US, people will assume that you are not actually in line and will cut in front of you (and remember—it's very rude to point out that they are being rude!). Conversations will take place at a much closer distance as well. I really don't like to be touched and need a good distance between me and whomever I am speaking with in order to feel comfortable. More than once I found myself backing up trying to establish the distance, with the speaker following me until I was literally up against the wall. Losing your temper in public is highly frowned upon as it results in a loss of face for both you and the person that you are speaking to.

When motioning for someone to join you, the acceptable gesture is with the palm facing down rather than up. Palms up is reserved for calling a prostitute. To indicate height (as in "My son is this tall"), the proper gesture is with the palm of the hand perpendicular to the ground as opposed to parallel, which is reserved for animals.

There is tremendous respect given to the elderly and to people with small children. Generally, anywhere where there is a line (paying a bill, for example) there will either be a designated line for the elderly and parents with small children or the guard will wave them to the front of the line when they enter.

Out and About: Traveling Around

Taxis, buses, and trolleys are the main means of transportation for tourists in Latin America. If you are taking a taxi, make sure that you are using a registered taxi with the registration number on the side. So-called "gypsy taxis" may be cheaper but are far more dangerous. It is generally acceptable to tip the driver—I usually just rounded the cost of the trip up to the nearest dollar when we lived in Ecuador.

Bus schedules are confusing, and a bus can take a very long time to get you from point A to point B. They are also very crowded most of the time. Interprovincial buses are dangerous, both mechanically and physically. Drivers are very lax about maintaining their buses, which means that the brakes go out regularly. This, coupled with their tendency to drive recklessly, results in bad accidents on a regular basis. If you are traveling between cities, I highly recommend that you contract a tour company with their own transportation. The cost will be higher, but it's worth it to potentially save your life.

Trollies are only in the big cities, and typically only run north to south. They are a very inexpensive way to get around, however, they are also a great place to get robbed. Be aware of your surroundings and don't assume that the sweet little old grandmother who is flirting with you is completely innocent—there's a good chance your wallet is now in her skirt pocket. Make sure that you pay attention to what is happening around you—many robberies begin by creating a distraction to divert your attention. Never accept anything on the street—drugs that can render you unable to control your actions can be infused into paper, flowers, or just about anything else that could potentially be handed out.

You will need to get vaccinations to visit most Central and Latin American countries. Yellow fever, malaria, typhoid and Hepatitis are the most common threats, and there are vaccines for all. Dengue, *Zika, and Chikungunya have been in the news lately, and unfortunately, there is no vaccine for these illnesses—you must take precautions to keep from contracting them. Use "jungle strength" bug repellent (you can get it at any Army-Navy store, or online) and wear long pants and long sleeves when at all possible. *Zika has been shown to be especially dangerous for pregnant women.

When you are traveling by plane, keep in mind that while security may not be as tight as you are used to, the "TSA" for the country you are in will still have a very low tolerance for anything out of the ordinary. Just as a little public service announcement...no matter what country you are in, or what language they speak...every airport worker on the planet knows the word "bomb". Don't make jokes about having one in your backpack or suitcase or whatever unless you want to get real up close and personal with the local authorities, who may or may not take a very long time to finally let you go after they figure out that it was a very unfunny joke. If your dimwitted traveling companion decides to make jokes, it might be wise to pretend you don't know them for a while. You have our permission to smack them later.

Things to Know

You will most likely need to convert your money into the local currency (the exception to this rule is Ecuador, which is on the American dollar). Do not convert all of your cash at once, as it can be difficult to convert it back, and don't carry everything you have with you at all times. Change is very hard to come by, so make sure that you carry small bills. *Travelers checks are generally not accepted by most institutions—

don't take them with you! Larger stores will accept credit cards. There is usually a fee involved for a credit card transaction, and fraud is common, so be very careful and know that you use them at your own risk. There are ATMs all over Latin America, but it is important to be very observant of the machine that you are using, as well as your surroundings. Check with your bank in the US to ensure that you will be able to withdraw cash while you are there—sometimes it can be difficult to find a machine that allows you to do so.

Many people in Central and Latin America speak or at least understand, some English. They will not always let you know this. We always told people that they needed to assume that everyone around them understood everything they were saying...so BE NICE. Don't say anything that you wouldn't want to be understood...because chances are someone within earshot knows exactly what you're saying.

Women traveling alone may find themselves receiving unwanted attention—mostly in the form of catcalls and suggestive remarks. It is advisable not to walk alone after dark, and be aware of your surroundings at all times. In larger cities where North American tourists are a relatively common sight, you will most likely receive less attention that you will if you venture out into the smaller cities and towns.

Southeast Asia

Southeast Asia includes Thailand, Cambodia, Laos, Vietnam, Indonesia, The Philippines, Myanmar, Brunei, Malaysia, East Timor, and Singapore. While there are many unique characteristics to each of these countries, there are some things that are "culturally universal".

Social Norms

The Asian culture is group-focused rather than individual-focused, and decisions are rarely made without the consultation and approval of family members. There is a high level of importance placed on bringing honor to the family name. They are generally a warm, inviting people and love to interact with those around them.

Where North Americans think of time as linear..."I have an appointment at 10:00, during which I expect to accomplish A, B, C...", time in the Asian culture is cyclical. "Yes, we have an appointment at 10:00 (and they will be 15-30 minutes early for the said appointment) but there are many things to consider before we can accomplish our goal, and if we don't accomplish it today, there will be another chance tomorrow." This can be very frustrating to the North American who needs to accomplish his task in order to move on to the next thing. Taking the time to learn about the culture in which you intend to work will help both of you understand and achieve success.

The people are relatively conservative in both manner and dress, especially in countries where Islam and Buddhism are the chief religions, and it is especially important to observe the rules of conduct when visiting places of worship. These include not taking pictures (it is considered quite offensive to take a picture of a statue of Buddha), speaking softly and making sure that you are dressed appropriately. Women (if they are permitted to enter at all) should wear modest, loose-fitting clothing that covers their shoulders and extends past their knees. Men should have on long pants and a collared shirt.

Losing your temper or creating a public scene is quite rude, and will cause the people around you to lose respect for you. If you are yelling at someone or making a scene, you will automatically be put into the same category as small children and animals, who are not able to control their emotions. A soft voice and reasonable demeanor will help to solve issues much more effectively than losing your cool.

Meeting and Greeting

The Western handshake has become relatively familiar in Asia, however, it is best to observe those around you and follow their lead when you meet someone. The Asian people greet each other with a "wai", which is a formal bow. There is a great deal of significance placed on doing it properly—the correct height, correct placement of the hands, etc. Unless you've been in the country for some time and have learned to do it properly, it is best to not do it all, in order to avoid offense. In Islamic countries, it is considered improper for women and men who are not related by either blood or marriage to touch one another, even in a casual greeting. Buddhist monks may not touch or be touched by a woman (even accidentally) without having to then undergo a cleansing ritual.

When you enter someone's home, you should remove your shoes as a sign of respect. When greeting someone, offering a gift or eating a meal, always use your right hand. The left hand is traditionally used for personal functions, and it is considered impolite, if not downright gross, to use your left hand in polite society.

Time to Eat!

Someone once told me that if you want to really understand a culture, observe how they celebrate birth, marriage, and death. I would add sharing a meal to this list. No matter what your cultural background is, food is an integral part of who you are. In Southeast Asian countries, sharing a meal is considered an honor. If you are invited to someone's home for a meal, it is considered rude to decline. A small gift for your host is always welcome—fruit, wine, and chocolate are popular choices. The gift will be well received, but not opened in front of you in order to save face should the recipient not care for it. Your host will indicate where you are to sit—it is important to wait for them to do so, in order to avoid any missteps. The oldest person in the room generally eats first, and proper etiquette dictates that you wait until they have begun to eat before starting your own meal. If you are using chopsticks, don't play with them or use them to stab your food. Your host will continue to refill your plate, so if you are full, it is acceptable to leave food on the plate to indicate that you are finished.

Street food is readily available in Asia and is not only delicious but relatively safe. Be aware of your surroundings—if you are in a slum area then it is probably not advisable to eat off of the street, but in heavily populated or touristy areas, you are most likely very safe. Asian food tends to be spicier than the Western diet, so take it easy at first to avoid shocking your system.

Phone Etiquette

Cell phones are very common in Asia, as in most of the rest of the world. It is generally considered rude to answer your phone in a public place (again, it is a "group-focused" culture, and your ringing cell phone can disturb the comfort level of the group) in order to keep from disturbing those around you. It is also considered rude to take your attention away from the person you are with to answer your phone—implying that the person on the phone is more important than the person in front of you. Phones should never be used in places of worship, even in silent mode. They should be turned off completely until you exit the building.

Gift Giving

Gift giving is a popular practice, but it is important to know the "rules" in order to avoid offending someone. In many countries, the color white signifies mourning, and should never be used to wrap a gift. Certain gifts, such as handkerchiefs, are associated with the dead, or the practice of mourning and should be avoided. (Does anyone actually use handkerchiefs anymore?) Gifts are never opened in the presence of the giver—this saves face in case the recipient doesn't like the gift.

Body Language

The Asian culture is very reserved, and children are taught from infancy to practice self-control. Although someone may be smiling at you, the most likely reason is that they either don't understand what you said, or they are embarrassed by something that you've just said or done. In our North American culture, we are taught to make eye contact with someone when we are talking to them, however in the Asian culture, this is a sign of disrespect, especially if a younger person looks an older person in the eye. When I was teaching at an international school, the Asian children would not look their teachers in the eye when they were talking to them. New teachers had to be educated on the cultural basis for this, as the children were often labeled as "disrespectful" when in fact the opposite was true.

The sole of the foot is considered to be unclean and should never be pointed directly at someone (for example, sitting with legs crossed) as this is a sign of disrespect. And while the foot is considered unclean, the head is the most sacred part of the body, as it is thought that this is where the person's spirit lives. For this reason, it is extremely rude to touch another person's head. This applies to both adults and children.

Travel Tips

Travel is very inexpensive in Asia, with buses and "tuk tuks" (a bicycle taxi) being the chief mode of transportation. Flights within the region are also very reasonable if you use regional carriers. Hotels and hostels can be found for just a few dollars a night. The region is generally safe for travelers, but be aware of your surroundings. Most of the time, safety is a matter of common sense—don't go out alone at night, don't let strangers buy you drinks, don't "flash your cash" when making purchases.

You will be able to use your bargaining skills to get good prices when you are using buses or tuk tuks. Westerners are generally seen as wealthy, and the prices automatically jump for a Western face. A little polite bargaining (remember—don't lose your temper) will usually bring the price down to one that is reasonable to both of you. *Please remember that the people you are dealing with have families to support, and this is their livelihood. While bargaining is perfectly acceptable, do not try to force them to give you ridiculously low prices. You will literally be taking food out of their children's mouths.

Women traveling alone in Asia are, as a rule, very safe. The quiet, reserved culture means that you won't even be subjected to catcalls or verbal harassment (there is always the chance—we are speaking in general terms here). Women are not always accorded the same level of respect in the Asian culture, however, for the most part, you will be able to travel and enjoy the beautiful countries with little or no problems. As always, make sure you are aware of your surroundings at all times, and use good judgment when out and about.

Things to Know

The easiest way to manage your money is to use the ATM. They dispense cash in the local currency, and your bank will automatically make the conversion when they deduct the money from your account. Some machines charge as much as $5 per transaction so you may need to shop around until you find the one with the lowest fees. Enterprising thieves, will, as always, find a way to attach devices to ATMs to swipe your card number, so make sure that you use machines in well-populated areas and keep an eye on your bank account. It is still possible to exchange money at the airport, but the exchange rates are not as favorable.

Stall keepers will expect you to bargain with them. This is part of the culture, and believe it or not, as long as you are not rude or demanding, they actually enjoy the interaction. Most prices will automatically rise for your Western face (in Ecuador we called it the "gringo tax") and by bargaining, you'll most likely get the prices back down to what the locals would pay. Again, remember that this is how people feed their families, so don't be a schmuck. If you aren't sure what a fair price would be and don't have any local friends that could help you, you can try buying the same thing at several locations to see what the price differences are.

Africa

Africa is the second largest continent in the world, with almost 12 million square miles, 54 independent countries and more than 1 billion people. This vast size means that there is no one African "culture" that could be considered universal. Cultural traditions vary with what country you are in, whether you are in the north (predominantly Muslim) or south (predominantly Christian and tribal), visiting a city or out in the bush. There are some things that are fairly common everywhere so we'll try to help you understand those, and give you some tips for traveling in both the northern and southern parts of the continent.

Social Structure

The African people are, with few exceptions, oriented toward the good of the group rather than the needs of the individual. Elders are venerated, and children are indulged, and both are treated with a mix of reverence and tolerance within society.

Time is a fluid concept, and being in a hurry will only serve to frustrate you. As in Latin America, it's more about the relationship than it is about the event, and nothing ever starts on time. Learning to "go with the flow" will help you to relax and enjoy your time rather than focusing on the "next thing".

Meeting and Greeting

North Africa is predominantly Muslim, with a Middle Eastern influence. It is important to greet people correctly in order to avoid offending someone—or worse. A woman who touches a man that she is not directly related to—even accidentally—can be severely punished. Never try to shake a woman's hand or hug her. With men, a Western-style handshake is generally acceptable. When in doubt, be observant and follow the people around you.

The influence in Southern Africa is more European. A Western style greeting—a handshake—is the typical greeting for both men and women. Again, if you aren't sure, you can ask someone or observe what is happening around you.

No matter where you are in Africa, you will find that the people are generally warm and friendly, and love to strike up a conversation. Allowing yourself to be open to this will greatly enrich your time in Africa, and you'll find that you meet the most amazing people.

When I was in South Africa, I discovered that everyone I met immediately wanted to be Facebook friends and get my address and cell phone number so that we could "keep in touch". This wasn't just the people that we were interacting with on our trip—the requests came from perfect strangers. It's probably a good idea not to give out this information. I accepted a couple of people on Facebook that were from a conference that I spoke at, but everyone else I just quietly passed on. It isn't necessary to make a big deal about it—just smile and change the subject.

Meal Time

No matter where you are, you'll find an abundance of tantalizing street food that delights your senses and makes your mouth water. If you choose to eat off of the street, just be careful. Anything that doesn't have to be cooked (juices, cut up fruit, etc.) should be avoided, as should thin-skinned fruits that you don't peel (apples, strawberries). Make sure that your meat is cooked to at least medium-well and don't eat raw vegetables, and enjoy! In South Africa, I was able to try crocodile, ostrich, kudu, impala, and warthog...and while I probably wouldn't hunt them down at my local market (no pun intended) I loved the chance to try new and different foods as part of my experience!

Traveling Around

Whether you choose to travel by bus, taxi, car, minivan or plane, it's safe to say that traveling in Africa won't be boring. In South Africa, they drive on the left side of the road, which means that your North American mind will be panicking every time your driver makes a left turn into traffic, and you'll wonder why he's not making a right on red. (Then you'll return to the US and your husband will ban you from driving until he's re-explained the rules of the road to you because you adapted a little too easily to driving on the right. Oops.)

If you choose to take a bus or minivan or car between countries, be aware of the border crossing requirements for the countries that you are crossing. For some countries, you may have to get out of the vehicle and cross on foot (the vehicle will be allowed to cross—just not with you in it) and then get back in and go on your merry way.

Public buses are probably your least safe mode of transportation between countries. They will be overly crowded, poorly maintained, not insured and just generally uncomfortable. You'll also run more of a risk of being robbed if you use a public bus. Private transportation will cost more, but it's worth it for the safety factor.

Body Language

In the African culture, it is considered rude for a young person to make eye contact with an elder, and sustained eye contact between any two people is considered a threat. If you are in an area that sees a lot of tourists, you are less likely to offend someone—they may not agree with your actions, but they will just chalk it up to you being a foreigner.

Because gestures can mean different things in different cultures, it's a good idea not to use them while you are traveling. Something like the "A-

OK" sign that is perfectly fine in the US could get you a good beating, or worse, in another country.

The African "personal bubble" is quite a bit smaller than the typical North American bubble, and people don't think twice about being right on top of you during a conversation. Little children are going to want to touch you—especially your hair because it is so different. I was working at a daycare in Cape Town, and the little girls there were especially fascinated with my hair and played with it the whole time I was there. At one point as my friend and I were letting them play, I heard (stage whisper) "Hey! Go get the brushes!" The other little cherub disappeared into the garden shed and came out with two toy rakes! Beauty parlor came to an abrupt end, as we drew the line at having our hair raked!

Phone Etiquette

Most African cell phones are on a pre-paid plan, which means that time=money. Cell phone calls are short and sweet—you come to the point immediately, without idle chitchat or niceties. It's important to realize that trying to chat with someone will waste their minutes, and it's possible that they don't have the money to replace them right away, so be considerate when calling.

Gift Giving

Unlike Latin America and Asia, where gifts are not opened in front of the giver, in Africa, the gift is opened immediately so that the recipient can express gratitude to the giver right away. Gifts are typically given at birthdays and Christmas, and are usually of a practical nature.

Things to Know

Again, Africa is so vast and has so many countries and cultures that it is difficult to come up with "blanket" customs. Researching your destination country will go a long way toward helping you to have an enjoyable visit without causing undue distress to those that you interact with during your time there.

The Middle East

The Middle East is rich in culture and tradition and contains many historical sites for Christians, Jews, and Muslims. It is also probably the most difficult part of the world to visit, due to the unrest and violence that has plagued the region for decades. While the majority of people are open and friendly, extremist groups are operating freely, and Westerners have been arrested and severely punished for what would be considered a minor breach of etiquette in their own country.

Social Structure

The Middle Eastern culture is based on mutual trust, relationship, and respect. Strong emphasis is placed on your word as bond, so it's very important not to make promises that you either cannot or do not intend to keep. A handshake when making a business transaction is considered far more trustworthy than even the most carefully executed business document, and it is a matter of honor to keep your word.

Modest, loose clothing is considered appropriate...tight, suggestive clothing is not. Women may need to cover their hair or in some cases wear a veil. Whether it is part of your religious beliefs or not, try to remember that you are the guest and not conforming is very insulting. Many people that I know who travel to the Middle East regularly carry a scarf with them in their purse so that they always have it if they need it.

PDA is absolutely taboo, and in some countries may actually get you arrested. Men and women—even if they are married—should refrain from touching in public. You will often see men holding hands with men and women holding hands with women—this is acceptable and does not have the same meaning that it does in the West.

Meeting and Greeting

As in Latin American countries, when you enter a room, you must greet each person in turn. The traditional greeting is salaam aleikum (peace be with you) however Westerners are not expected to know this, and may simply say "hello" when greeting everyone. Older people are treated with the utmost respect and should always be greeted first in a social situation.

A handshake is acceptable between men, however, a man should never extend his hand to a woman. In the Islamic culture, women are prohibited from touching a man that they are not directly related to. Although this has been relaxed somewhat in the business world, it is still always best to follow their lead. If a woman wishes to shake your hand, she will extend hers first.

In the Middle East, perhaps more so than anywhere else in the world, religion is a very touchy subject. Most Middle Eastern countries are Muslim, and many prohibit any type of conversation or activity that could be construed as proselytizing. It is permitted to tell someone that you are a Christian if you are asked, but do not take the conversation in a direction that could make someone feel as though you are trying to convert them. Atheism is not well understood here—if you are asked about your religion and you are an atheist, it is better to answer "I am a seeker" as this denotes an interest in spiritual matters, rather than disbelief.

Dining Etiquette

There is a heavy emphasis placed on hospitality, and it's quite rude to decline an invitation to dine either in a restaurant or in someone's home. In most homes, you'll be asked to remove your shoes before entering. When you enter the dining area, always wait for your host to indicate where he would like for you to sit, as there is a social protocol to be followed.

Always use your right hand for anything related to dining and food. The left hand is for taking care of matters related to hygiene and is considered very unclean. In many Middle Eastern homes and restaurants, the food is served from a communal dish in the center of the table and diners use pieces of bread to scoop their food. Using your left hand will contaminate the entire dish and insult your host.

You will probably be served foods that are unfamiliar to you...eat them anyway. Refusing to do so, even politely, is an insult to your host. Barring life-threatening food allergies, which most of us don't have, eating something once won't kill you. You might even find out you like it.

Body Language

Remember—hand signals that are perfectly fine in the West can have completely different meanings elsewhere. Never use that "A-OK" sign in the Middle East. It's an insult and can earn you a good beating. Keep your feet flat on the floor, as crossing your ankle over your knee is insulting—the bottom of the foot is considered to be the most unclean place on the body, and it is rude to point it at someone.

Eastern Europe

Eastern Europe is made up of Russia, the Czech Republic, the Ukraine, Romania, Bulgaria, Hungary, Croatia, and Poland. The region is rich in history, with beautiful churches and mosques in every country. The many languages spoken throughout the region are all Slavic in origin, with some countries using the Latin alphabet and others keeping with tradition and using Cyrillic characters.

Social Structure

The Eastern European countries suffered heavily during WWI and WWII. They all, at one time or another, lived under either a Communist or Fascist regime, and there are many people alive today who still remember those dark days in their history. The traditions and superstitions of the people go back thousands of years and are a vibrant and rich part of their heritage.

Meeting and Greeting

Many Eastern Europeans are a part of the Orthodox church, and take very seriously the Biblical mandate to greet one another with a "holy kiss". Traditionally, men greet men and women greet women—intergender kissing is not practiced. It is not unusual for a man to kiss another man on the lips, however for a Westerner it can be a bit of a shock! A pastor friend of mine was visiting Russia. His host pastor met him at the airport, and my friend was a bit shocked when his host pastor came in for a kiss! My friend tried to simultaneously dodge the kiss and back away until he was up against the wall looking like a bobbing chicken with nowhere to go! A firm handshake is an acceptable greeting, although don't be surprised if you get the handshake AND a holy kiss.

Dining Etiquette

Eastern Europeans are hospitable, and the comfort and enjoyment of their guests is very important. When dining, the most honored guest eats first, and everyone else follows suit. If you aren't sure, always follow the lead of your host. Your drink will be refilled every time your glass falls below half empty, so if you don't want any more, make sure you leave it at least half full! (Side note—this is also the custom in many Latin American countries. A pastor friend of mine was visiting Argentina. He landed about 10:00 at night and his hosts took him to dinner. He wasn't a drinker but didn't want to be rude, so he finished all of the wine that was offered to him throughout the evening. When he stood up to leave the restaurant about 2 am, he fell over!)

Bread will be served at every meal. It is considered unlucky not to finish all of the bread that you take, so make sure you don't take more than you can eat. Toasts will be offered throughout the meal—always maintain eye contact when making a toast, from the time you raise your glass until you set it back down on the table, as it is rude not to do so. It is also rude to refuse or decline a toast if asked to make one.

Traveling Around

Taxis, buses, and trains are all acceptable ways to travel throughout Eastern Europe. Learning a few words in your host language will go a long way towards making sure that you get an acceptable fare, as it's not usual for the driver to "misunderstand" and take you to your destination via the "scenic route". All things considered, you most likely still won't pay very much for your ride (at least by our standards), so you'll come out ahead in the end. It is common practice to round your fare to the next even amount as a tip as well.

Body Language

Eastern Europeans, like most of the rest of the world, have a smaller "personal bubble" than most North Americans. Physical touch is a common part of interactions. One thing that always throws Westerners for a loop is the head shaking in Eastern Europe. We are used to a side-to-side motion of the head signifying "no" and an up-and-down motion meaning "yes". It is exactly the opposite in Eastern European countries, and so make sure that you pay attention when talking to someone so that you don't get confused about his answer!

Unlike many parts of the world, gifts are usually opened immediately in order to express gratitude to the giver. If you are giving gifts to a newborn baby, make sure you give an odd number of gifts, as even numbers are considered unlucky. Taking a small gift to a host or hostess is acceptable, but make sure it is something not terribly expensive, as this could convey to the recipient that he or she is "too poor" to afford nice things.

Things to Know

As many Eastern Europeans still remember the harsh regimes under which they were forced to live, it is in extremely poor taste to mention their historical past to them. Even younger people had parents and grandparents who remember it vividly and will not want to discuss it. They love to talk about their countries but allow them to take the lead when it comes to this type of conversation.

General Travel Tips

No matter where you are going, there are some things that are good to remember when traveling.

*You are the visitor. You have chosen to visit your host country, and you owe the people the respect that comes with being a visitor. You wouldn't walk into someone's home in your passport country and be demanding and rude (at least we hope you wouldn't) and you shouldn't do it in your host country either. Open your mind and allow yourself to embrace the new culture. Try new foods, learn a new dance, take a class in the local language.

*Different does not mean wrong. Just because the customs of your host country are different than what you are used to, that doesn't mean they are wrong. The words "But in the US, we...) are rude and insensitive. And if we might be blunt...people don't care how we do things in the US. They are usually thinking "Well if you like it so much you're welcome to return!"

*Your embassy cannot do much for you. I heard the words "If I get in trouble, the embassy will..." over and over while I lived overseas. The reality is that your embassy cannot...and will not...interfere if you are arrested in your host country, especially if you were actually breaking the law. The most you can expect is that they will send someone to where you are detained to make sure that your physical needs are being met. They cannot guarantee a fair trial, and they cannot get you out of jail. In short, behave yourself.

*Penalties for illegal drugs are swift and often brutal. While your favorite recreational drug might be readily available, know that in many countries, even a small amount can cost you dearly...up to and including your life. It's not worth it. Don't transport it, don't try to buy it and don't use it...it's not worth it. And see the previous point if you have any questions about your embassy and their willingness to help.

*This bears repeating. No matter where you are in the world, people know and understand the word "bomb". Don't joke about it. Don't try to be funny. It's not worth the moment of juvenile humor that you might get from it. Just, don't.

This world is an amazing and beautiful place, and if you are willing to broaden your horizons, you will find that each country that you visit occupies a little piece of your heart long after you've left. You've taken the first step...you have a passport...now to explore and enjoy and allow yourself to be changed, one country at a time!

Printed in the USA
CPSIA information can be obtained
at www.ICGtesting.com
LVHW090159211024
794370LV00007B/213